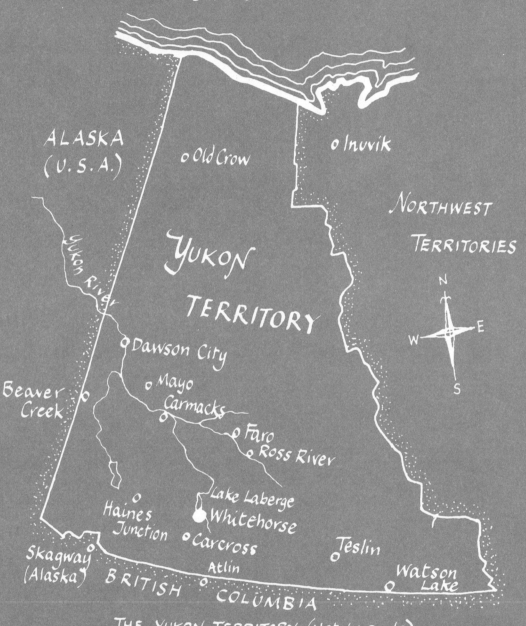

THE YUKON TERRITORY (Not to scale)
Position of main towns are approximate.

THE
CREMATION OF SAM McGEE

BY ROBERT W. SERVICE

PAINTINGS BY TED HARRISON

INTRODUCTION BY PIERRE BERTON

GREENWILLOW BOOKS, NEW YORK

Library of Congress Cataloging-in-Publication Data
Service, Robert W. (Robert William), 1874-1958.
The cremation of Sam McGee.
Summary: Constantly suffering from the cold,
Sam makes his companion on the Arctic trail
promise to cremate him when he dies, which
the companion does—to his great surprise.
1. Children's poetry, Canadian.
[1. Yukon Territory—Poetry.
2. Narrative poetry.   3. Canadian poetry]
I. Harrison, Ted, 1926-   ill.
II. Title. PR9199. 3.S45C7 1987
811'.52   86-14971
ISBN 0-688-06903-7

This book is dedicated to the memory of the late Jim Murdock, co-founder of "The Frantic Follies." Jim's vision and energy kept alive the spirit of the sourdoughs and created a unique stage version of "The Cremation of Sam McGee" that continues to delight thousands of visitors to the Yukon.

This book represents a happy marriage between the most eloquent of the Yukon poets and the most brilliant of the Yukon artists. Robert W. Service and Edward Hardy Harrison have more than that in common: both were born in England; both roamed the world; both were caught up by what Service called "the spell of the Yukon." No one caught that spell in words better than Service; no painter has captured the particular essence of the Yukon experience better than Harrison.

The work of both men is in the romantic tradition. Service, the outsider who'd roamed the continent, wrote his best work a decade after the gold rush and much of it before he'd even seen the Klondike. Harrison, the newcomer, who had served in the army in England, India, Egypt, Kenya, Uganda, and Somaliland and would serve later in Malaysia and New Zealand, was better able to appreciate the peculiar essence of the North. His painting style is unique: part Oriental, part native Indian, part Ted Harrison.

In their work, both men caught the color that the native Yukoner sometimes fails to see because he's too familiar with the land and the people: Service's poetry is always more than colorful; like Harrison's many-hued paintings, it can also be surrealistic. This is especially true of "The Cremation of Sam McGee." Service's poems can be hard boiled and realistic (as in "The Man from Eldorado" or "Clancy of the Mounted"), but the ones he wrote in Whitehorse, before he reached the Klondike, have a mythic quality. Both men, I think, are affected by the mystique of the northern lights—the jiggling aurora that dances across the sky. These ever-expanding multicolored ripples—which, in Service's famous phrase, "have seen queer sights"—are an essential part of the Harrison style.

Sam McGee was a real person, a customer at the Bank of Commerce where Service worked. The *Alice May* was a real boat (the *Olive May*), a derelict on Lake Laberge. The rest is pure Service. It was his second published poem—the first was "The Shooting of Dan McGrew." Service, I think, mourned the fact that nothing he wrote afterwards was ever as famous as these two classics.

But of the two, "Sam McGee" is authentic Yukon while "Dan McGrew" is pure American-style Wild West. It's a poem about a subject that is familiar to every Northerner—the subject of cold and what cold can do to a man. It's interesting that although the color of cold is usually thought to be blue or white, Ted Harrison's Northern paintings fairly vibrate with all the colors of the rainbow. It is as if he is determined to banish cold with these hot paintings.

Harrison mixes his palette the way Matisse did—with no regard to conventional rules; and yet the colors do not clash. Oranges and pinks, golden yellows and chartreuses march side by side in perfect harmony, like the Arctic poppies that grow along the banks of the Yukon River in the ghost towns of another era.

There is humor in Harrison's work, as there is in Service's. "Sam McGee" is essentially a funny poem, and if it's recited with style and verve it will draw a laugh— as it should. I've never heard Harrison recite Service; but his rendition of "Sam Small," in a broad Lancashire accent, is a classic. So are his cartoons.

It is a joy to see these two unique talents combined. They have so much in common: a sense of discovery, a brashness, and a feeling of *joie de vivre* that is to be heard in the driving force of the Service narratives and seen in the dazzling vibrations of the Harrison art. There is, however, one difference: Service fled the Yukon in 1912 for the hot sun of Monte Carlo, never to return. Harrison, who's had plenty of hot sun in the colonial subtropics, has clearly put his roots down in his adopted North. For that we should all be grateful.

PIERRE BERTON
KLEINBURG, ONTARIO, CANADA, 1986

As a youth the first mountains I encountered were man-made piles of stony waste, the refuse from the grimy coal mine that dominated our small Durham village. Its sooty smoke and microscopic dust were our constant companions as we played, studied, worshipped, and slept. It even entered our souls, for we all realized that Heaven was far removed from the environment in which all of us existed. Hadn't we been taught that the angels themselves were clothed in purest white raiment? Surely such splendor could not remain in pristine condition for long if a pit village were its home. Even the Pearly Gates themselves would have appeared drab in such surroundings.

Thus we learned to escape in a realm of fantasy conjured up by our vivid imaginations, nourished by the Saturday afternoon cinema matinée at the Palace, which overlooked the very slag heap I have described. The silver screen joined forces with the school library to carry us to lands whose names became signposts on the route to paradise. Hopalong Cassidy joined forces with R. L. Stevenson and Jack London to introduce us to this other world, not heard of in chapel but nevertheless heavenly in its message. Especially stirring were the stories "White Fang" and "Call of the Wild," with the robust adventure-filled verses of Robert W. Service. Their words illuminated the darkness of ignorance and kindled the flame of adventure that led me to seek a refuge "far from the madding crowd's ignoble strife." They told of a land all white and elementally pure where a person could gaze upon mountains fashioned by God, not torn from the bowels of the earth by sweated labor.

Eventually, during my adult wanderings, I came upon this land of the North and settled down with my family to savor its wonders. It has indeed fulfilled all expectations. In summer and fall the creeks come alive, pouring their waters into glistening mirror-like lakes, which again drain into mighty tumbling rivers heading towards the great Arctic Seas. Vast forests of spruce and poplar carpet the feet of mountains whose crests remain shrouded in caps of eternal ice. Winter covers all the land in a white carpet of powdery snow, which swirls to the rhythm of fresh invigorating winds. In the crisp clear air the sound of a homesteader's ax or the bark of a husky dog can travel for miles. Even today relatively few people inhabit this vast wilderness.

Much of the Yukon has changed since Robert W. Service lived here, but were he to return, there is much that he would recognize. The lively hospitable spirit of the people, the hiss of sled runners over the crisp snow, and the barking of the huskies as they mush their way along familiar trails. Ravens continue to tumble in the clear winter sky and tease the household dogs, who vie with them for the rich pickings of garbage cans. One can still stir to the haunting cry of wolf and loon through desolate valleys and over remote lakes. Lake Laberge continues to fascinate both local and visitor alike with its vast waters surrounded by a fortress of hills. The winds can blow it into a stormy frenzy but, standing on the shore, one can easily visualize the smoky plume emanating from the boiler of the *Alice May* as Sam McGee begins to thaw out.

The Yukon continues to weave its spell and remains a magnet to those travelers who prefer to see a few sparkling bubbles in the wine of life. Indeed, the magic of Service's verse becomes much more meaningful as one gazes upon the land he knew intimately. There remain a few places on this earth that still satisfy the imagination and nourish the soul. Such a place is the Yukon.

Welcome to the world of Robert W. Service, and to the spirit of the land that inspired him.

Ted Harrison

TED HARRISON
WHITEHORSE, CANADA, 1986

There are strange things done

               in the midnight sun

   By the men who moil for gold;

The Arctic trails have their secret tales

   That would make your blood run cold;

The Northern Lights

       have seen queer sights,

   But the queerest they ever did see

Was that night on the marge of Lake Lebarge

         I cremated Sam McGee.

The *Alice May* lies embedded in the ice of Lake Laberge. In the distance lie the hills of the eastern shore while in the foreground can be seen the estuaries of the Yukon River as it enters the lake. Above the narrator glow the northern lights, serving to illuminate the scene.

Now Sam McGee was from Tennessee,
    where the cotton blooms and blows.
Why he left his home in the South to roam 'round the Pole,
    God only knows.
He was always cold, but the land of gold seemed to hold him
    like a spell;
Though he'd often say in his homely way that
    "he'd sooner live in hell."

On a Christmas Day
    we were mushing our way over the Dawson trail.
Talk of your cold! through the parka's fold
    it stabbed like a driven nail.
If our eyes we'd close, then the lashes froze till
    sometimes we couldn't see;
It wasn't much fun, but the only one to whimper
    was Sam McGee.

Sam sits tightly blanketed in the sled as it passes a typical Dawson City dwelling. The dog team is harnessed in line while the children watch them enter the wilderness beyond the town.

And that very night, as we lay packed tight
    in our robes beneath the snow,
And the dogs were fed,
    and the stars o'erhead were dancing heel and toe,
He turned to me, and "Cap,"says he,
   "I'll cash in this trip, I guess;
And if I do, I'm asking that you won't refuse
    my last request."

On a clear cold winter night the stars twinkle with an exceptional brilliance. To lie together with their bags in the snow gives added insulation and comfort. Even the leaping snowshoe rabbit fails to excite the surfeited sled dogs.

Well, he seemed so low that I couldn't say no;
    then he says with a sort of moan:
"It's the cursèd cold, and it's got right hold till
    I'm chilled clean through to the bone.
Yet 'tain't being dead—
    it's my awful dread of the icy grave that pains;
So I want you to swear that, foul or fair,
    you'll cremate my last remains."

A pal's last need is a thing to heed,
    so I swore I would not fail;
And we started on at the streak of dawn; but God!
    he looked ghastly pale.
He crouched on the sleigh, and he raved all day
    of his home in Tennessee;
And before nightfall a corpse was all that was left
    of Sam McGee.

Dawn in the Yukon can be a most glorious sight. The river and lake glow like molten gold as the sun rises over the hills of the Klondike. The land, however, remains in the icy grip of winter.

There wasn't a breath in that land of death,
and I hurried, horror driven,
With a corpse half hid that I couldn't get rid,
because of a promise given;
It was lashed to the sleigh, and it seemed to say:
"You may tax your brawn and brains,
But you promised true, and it's up to you to
cremate those last remains."

Only the ravens are moving in the intense cold. Yet they crouch down so that their legs are protected by the enveloping feathers. It is so cold, and the snow is so powdery, that the trees remain dark as the slightest breeze dislodges the snow from their branches.

Now a promise made is a debt unpaid,
    and the trail has its own stern code.
In the days to come, though my lips were dumb,
    in my heart how I cursed that load.
In the long, long night,
    by the lone firelight, while the huskies,
    round in a ring,
Howled out their woes to the homeless snows—O God!
    how I loathed the thing.

The Yukon air is so dry that an old stove exposed to the elements will not easily rust. Often cabins can lie deserted for years with their contents intact and well preserved.

And every day that quiet clay
    seemed to heavy and heavier grow;
And on I went, though the dogs were spent
    and the grub was getting low;
The trail was bad,
    and I felt half mad, but I swore I would not give in;
And I'd often sing to the hateful thing, and
    it hearkened with a grin.

Till I came to the marge of Lake Lebarge,
    and a derelict there lay;
It was jammed in the ice,
    but I saw in a trice it was called the "Alice May."
And I looked at it, and I thought a bit, and
    I looked at my frozen chum;
Then "Here," said I, with a sudden cry,
    "is my cre-ma-tor-eum."

An ice-fog lies over the lake. It emanates from the unfrozen
river water, which can still flow in places despite an extremely
low temperature. Ultimately the paddlewheeler will totally
disintegrate save for the huge metal boilers.

Some planks I tore from the cabin floor,
    and I lit the boiler fire;
Some coal I found
    that was lying around, and I heaped the fuel higher;
The flames just soared, and the furnace roared—
    such a blaze you seldom see;
And I burrowed a hole in the glowing coal,
    and I stuffed in Sam McGee.

The paddlewheelers burned wood as a fuel, and numerous wood supply stations were placed at strategic intervals along the banks of the Yukon River. There would be more than enough around to cremate Sam.

Then I made a hike,
  for I didn't like to hear him sizzle so;
And the heavens scowled, and the huskies howled,
  and the wind began to blow.
It was icy cold, but the hot sweat rolled down my cheeks,
  and I don't know why;
And the greasy smoke in an inky cloak
  went streaking down the sky.

In the foreground stand the remains of a cache. These were
built to keep food out of the reach of animals such as bears and
wolves. Entrance was gained by climbing the ladder and
unlocking the small door placed below the raven. Many caches
are still in use.

I do not know how long in the snow
    I wrestled with grisly fear;
But the stars came out
    and they danced about ere again I ventured near;
I was sick with dread, but I bravely said:
    "I'll just take a peep inside.
I guess he's cooked, and it's time I looked,"
. . . then the door
    I opened wide.

The boilers generated tremendous heat and had to be stoked almost continually in order to keep up the pressure of steam. More wood would be required on the journey from Dawson City to Whitehorse as the boat was required to fight the current of the great Yukon River.

And there sat Sam,
    looking cool and calm, in the heart of the furnace roar;
And he wore a smile you could see a mile, and he said:
    "Please close that door.
It's fine in here,
    but I greatly fear you'll let in the cold and storm—
Since I left Plumtree, down in Tennessee,
    it's the first time I've been warm."

Sam is now in a state of bliss. His sole garment is a pair of red long johns, and the flowers of summer strew his imagination so that Lake Laberge and Plumtree, Tennessee, become synonymous.

There are strange things done
                              in the midnight sun
      By the men who moil for gold;
The Arctic trails have their secret tales
      That would make your blood run cold;
The Northern Lights
              have seen queer sights,
      But the queerest they ever did see
Was that night on the marge of Lake Lebarge
                              I cremated Sam McGee.

Here the placer miners wash the alluvial deposits of sand and gravel so that the gold nuggets, being heavy, fall to the base of the rocker box wielded by the miner on the left. As the nuggets are sluiced they become trapped in the riffles placed under the box and can be easily removed.

The typography was adapted from the original Canadian
edition designed by Peter Durham Dodd, MGDC.
The text type is Palatino.

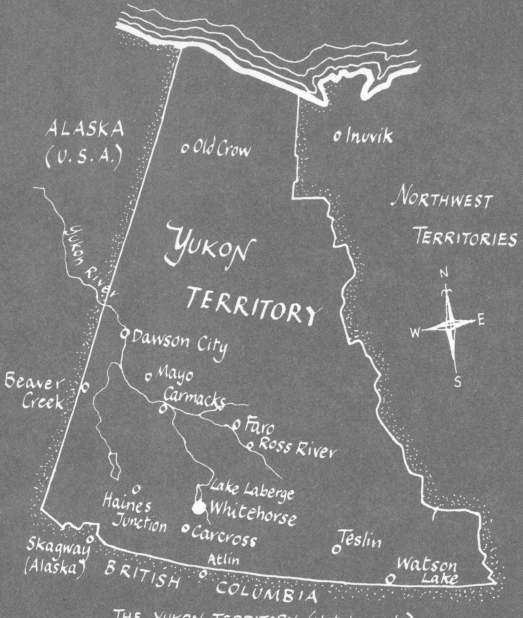

THE YUKON TERRITORY (Not to scale)
Position of main towns are approximate.